Eclectic
INTERIORS

ROOM *by* ROOM

GLOUCESTER MASSACHUSETTS

ROCKPORT PUBLISHERS

KATHRYN LIVINGSTON

First published in the United States of America by
Rockport Publishers, Inc.
33 Commercial Street
Gloucester, Massachusetts 01930-5089
Telephone: (978) 282-9590
Facsimile: (978) 283-2742

Distributed to the book trade and art trade in the United States by
North Light Books, an imprint of
F & W Publications
1507 Dana Avenue
Cincinnati, Ohio 45207
Telephone: (800) 289-0963

Other Distribution by
Rockport Publishers, Inc.
Gloucester, Massachusetts 01930-5089

ISBN 1-56496-426-4

10 9 8 7 6 5 4 3 2 1

Design: Argus Visual Communication, Boston
Cover Image: Sam Gray

Printed in China.

Dedication

Dedication

To my son and daughter, Bret and Valerie, who, through a nomadic way of growing up, are thoroughly cross-cultural beings.

Acknowledgments

Acknowledgments

I would like to express my deep-felt appreciation to the entire staff at Rockport Publishers, and especially to Rosalie Grattaroti, Acquisitions Editor, who conceived the *Room by Room* series and asked me to take on the *Eclectic* volume of the quartet. Her zest and savvy, her passion for good design, and her can-do attitude in general made working with her always a positive experience. Invaluable throughout was Martha Wetherill, the book's editor, who steered the project through a thicket of visual and verbal challenges. With her highly evolved tastes, fine-honed editorial instincts, and gracious ways, she was never less than inspiring. I'm also much indebted to copyeditor Madeline Perri for her skillful and sensitive shaping and sharpening of the text. Of course, elemental to a book about design is its own design. So that *Eclectic* would look whereof it speaks, Argus Visual Communications brought to its graphics infinite imagination and daring.

At the core of this book is the outpouring of talent by the many interior designers, architects, and photographers whose work appears on these pages. The creative sparks they throw off serves to illuminate the way to the astonishing possibilities open to eclectic rooms.

Finally, my special gratitude goes to Charles Patteson, major catalyst behind the fifth American Hospital of Paris French Designer Showhouse in New York, which brought together a glittering array of France's and America's most innovative designers. This hotbed of eclectic ideas and international style, which coincided with the initial stages of this book, led me to several of the key artists and decorative concepts featured here.

Contents

John F. Saladino *Foreword*

The overwhelming amount of information that we are exposed to daily through newspapers, television, computers, and fax machines, assault and test our instincts. As we carve a path through a cacophony of choices, we must rely on our instincts as much as our education to find a new order.

I have always said that it is more important what you leave out than what you put in. To make a beautiful environment is not unlike making choices from a menu. We would be in trouble if we ordered everything that a restaurant could provide. Choosing is about self-discipline. It's about editing out what is trendy and superficial, and ultimately inappropriate. It is a challenge, then, to edit out what may be compulsively satisfying but not correct in the long run.

I have always depended on scale as the omnipotent diverse orchestrator of styles and furnishings. Color also unifies very different cultural assemblages. The temptation is to revert to the shopping cart mentality and walk down the aisles of time and take a quart of Adam, four pounds of Santa Fe, and three pounds of Tudor revival. Financial indulgence is often the worst disease because it gives us access to too much, whereas we know that a budget will always extract a disciplined solution.

Scale, then, is the umbrella that can shelter and contain, and give order. The most unbelievable combinations are successful if they have a homogenous size and color. Huge lounge chairs, no matter how beautiful and comfortable, will make a small room look as silly as tight fitting clothes. Travel, for those who are fortunate enough to benefit from it, provides so many ideas and things to incorporate into our lives: Patio dining in Tunisia, where guests keep cool by soaking their toes in a common shallow pool under the table; the color of building materials in England, where stone and lead downspouts give us pause to think about how certain plants will look better against some materials and not others, may be wonderful experiences but not portable. Tudor revival houses in Arizona are inappropriate and silly. To be eclectic is better done indoors. There are a few rules in late-twentieth-century decorating and design, but it seems to me that we can only enjoy some things in museums and not try to recreate nostalgia where our interiors and our houses take on theme park settings.

Ultimately, to your materials be true! Don't be ashamed of vinyl. Let it be vinyl and not leatherette. If you like a French country kitchen, don't put in fiberglass beams. When you bring back the salt and pepper shakers from Guatemala, chances are they won't look good with grandmother's candelabra, but they would be wonderful at the next barbecue. Common sense, attention to scale, and the ability not to eat every style before you will keep you on the road to appropriate solutions.

Introduction

Kathryn Livingston

As eternally surprising and contradictory as modern life itself, eclectic interior design lets us inscribe our homes with our beliefs, our dreams, our stories.

The term *eclecticism* is derived from the Greek word *eklektikos*, meaning "gathering and selecting the best from a variety of sources." The idea holds a seductive appeal. Creatively, it allows us both seasoned reflection and intuitive immediacy. An eclectic approach satisfies our closely twined personal urges to hold on to our inherited culture while indulging our passion for reinvention—the freedom to be true to ourselves and to make things up as we go along. Both are powerful desires: nostalgia and the impulse to embrace change. As the Nobel-prize–winning poet Octavio Paz observed, "To be truly modern, we must be in touch with our traditions."

While this delicate juggling of comforting legacy and brave innovation is at the very heart of eclectic decorating, so is our seemingly growing need to personalize our private spaces. Never has home design been less concerned with matching fashionable colors or the latest window treatment than with the sincere desire to achieve that something called personal style and the wish to stamp our habitats with an individual signature.

With instant global communication, virtual around-the-world shopping, and the restless syncopation of highly diverse cultures all around us, our lives are richly nuanced by what was once quite foreign to us. We taste hybridized flavors and hear creolized sounds. In the realm of fine art we witness wondrous multimedia effects. We now know that aesthetic energy and verve come from a distinctive mix of disparate elements and that rooms filled with objects from a single period tend to be stiff and monotonous.

Inadvertently, as well as through travel, we have become a new breed of image and information collectors. To meld the exotic with the classic is now almost second nature to most of us. To fuse the high-tech with the antique is a nearly automatic sensory reflex. Our eyes connect the primitive and the refined artifact. Our instincts tell us that the demand for ease and the yearning for elegance need not cancel each other out. If it suits us, a rugged mountain bike can coexist with a haughty heirloom piano, just as a sleekly crafted wooden stool from Cameroon and an ornately gilded Empire period chair can share an intriguing rapport.

Nevertheless, funneling our wider world view into a sophisticated apartment or a truly original house can pose a challenge. Obviously, not everything goes with everything. Decorating rules may have been relaxed, but where to begin? How to combine furnishings for a fresh and exciting effect as well as create a physically comfortable and emotionally uplifting environment? Answers do not lie in a blueprint but spring from insights into specific decorating schemes—such as those presented in *Room by Room: Eclectic Interiors*.

With their educated explorers' eyes, the tastemaking designers and photographers whose works are featured on the following pages lead us into a series of stunning spaces that open up subtexts of eclectic style. They experiment with cross-cultural mixes, retro-techno fusion design, romantic modernism, stripped classicism, surrealistic wit, and highly personalized collections. In their stylish interiors, East meets West, old meets new, natural meets synthetic—with grace, hipness, and exuberance. Cool and restrained or sensual and bold, the most striking feature of these rooms is their sincerity of expression. Their creators trust what they like. That is their starting point. Their clever ideas draw from the forms, colors, textures, and proportions encountered in the paintings, sculpture, architecture of many periods, the wisdom of many cultures, and twentieth-century decorative arts icons. They show that light, space, daily use, and thematic kinship all work to transform an unorthodox mix into a coherent whole. They prove that the secret of eclectic style and that of personal signature are the same: knowing when to break the mold and when to honor the exemplary.

In recent years, a dash of humor and a pinch of irreverence have been tossed into the eclectic brew. Ordinary things can be made extraordinary by a playful wit. Surreal and trompe-l'oeil motifs, found objects and pop artifacts, outrageously displaced industrial tools fulfilling new decorative purposes— even if they sometimes puzzle as much as they please—have a way of creating lighthearted, young atmospheres. It's as if these arresting combinations want to poke fun at the self-consciously-decorated look itself. This improvisational attitude fits with the eclectic idiom. The idea today is to see beauty in modest things as well as in all the glittering prizes. As members of a highly mobile society, we prefer the fluidity of the touchably eclectic to the impersonal aura of staid luxe.

Eclectic Entrances

Whether a mudroom or an imposing hall with a sweeping staircase, whether an object-cluttered foyer in a sophisticated apartment or a breezy portico in a mellow clime, the eclectic entrance instantly presents clues about who lives in the home.

It may combine conceits from the past with fantasies of the future, but it is decidedly in the now. It reflects the life of the home's inhabitants and tells of individual experience. When most successful, the entrance reveals a personal image bank rich in visual elements linking cultures, space, and time.

The eclectic entryway greets with a certain surprise, setting the tone for unexpected blends of East and West, old and new, bold and subtle, natural materials and synthetics. It enlivens heirlooms by juxtaposing them with pop culture artifacts or tribal totems.

Whatever its size—a postage stamp by an elevator shaft or a high-ceilinged reception hall—the entrance is the first room seen on entering your house. Its decor sets the tone for the rest of your home. The shape of entrances is often tricky because of architectural necessities such as stairs. Such spaces lack the precise purpose of, say, kitchens or dining rooms, which have distinct requirements. Entrances, for all these reasons, may pose the biggest inspirational challenge in decorating, yet may be the most fun to create. By combining just a few objects in an individualistic grouping, you can reveal your signature right at the front door.

Often the space itself dictates what is required. Sometimes two styles of banisters meet in this spot. It could be riveting to emphasize their contrast through bold paint or lighting. On the other hand, a mix of furniture, art, coatracks, umbrella stands, and fabric or wallpaper could merge them into an organic unit. A bibliophile short of space might store favorite volumes in an entrance. An inveterate traveler could create a pagoda or tent effect to display treasures from afar, such as a mahogany Thai chair, a pre-Columbian animal carving from Central America, or a prized seventeenth-century French console. Collectors might showcase 1940s Coca-Cola posters, an antique musical instrument, a contemporary painting, or something handpainted on the wall itself by a friend.

Entrances should be inviting and interesting to walk through. Space, or lack of it, suggests the color scheme. The way light enters is a consideration when deciding whether the room should be airy and pale or cozy, with a darker palette. Often a strongly patterned rug or geometric floor provides the cue. Lighting fixtures can transform the mood. There should be a place to hang coats and, ideally, a spot where keys, gloves, and mail can be set down. An unusual mirror for last-minute grooming is an attractive idea and takes little space; in fact, it can add the illusion of more space than there really is.

The eclectic foyer can handle a wild array of eye-catching finds—Victorian bamboo shelves, antlered hanging devices for outerwear, wine racks, gaming tables, statues of Far-Eastern deities, potted trees. But remember—this is a heavy-traffic zone. Awkward protrusions can cause accidents during animated greetings.

Previous pages: A whiff of English country romance
pervades this second-floor reception area. Flowers,
floral chintz touches, and a lovingly assembled set
of Chinese screens, cabinets, and chairs convey this
feeling. Some fine examples of antique European
chinoiserie such as the mirror and the bamboo
settee complete the scene. Design: Killough Irwin,
courtesy of Rogers Memorial Library, Southampton
Designer Showhouse; Photo: Phillip H. Ennis

Utilizing color, texture, and scale to achieve
powerful dramatic impact, this sun-dappled,
barely furnished modern entrance hall incorporates both humble Mayan roofing, open to the
sky, and Colonial hacienda grandeur from
Mexico's rich architectural heritage. Design:
Manolo Mestre; Photo: Tim Street-Porter

An awkward corner bursts with personality as a result of an adventurous grouping that includes two twentieth-century paintings and an Art Nouveau mirror. The traces of gold on a pastel Italian chair lead the eye to a stunning console, fashioned from the frieze of a demolished building, that holds a collection of favorite books, tortoise boxes, and an inherited monogrammed vase. Design: Thomas Beeton; Photo: Tim Street-Porter

Here is country eclecticism distilled with an urban appreciation of simple pleasures: a spare entryway without curtains or rugs, only pristine walls and a marine-varnished floor. The functional beauty of the cottage door, the plain window, and the contrast of the twisted wrought-iron railing and the solitary chair—a repository for wildflowers—belie the sophistication of the treatment. Design: Brian Murphy, BAM Design; Photo: Tim Street-Porter

A disproportionately blown-up modern painting of a classical male face intriguingly dwarfs yet exaggerates the shock value of a small Spanish colonial sculpture of a pair of mystically gesturing hands. This entryway pulls the outdoors in through a poetic layering of cobblestones, marble, fieldstone, and brick. Rough wooden beams and ladders play against sleek walls of glass and glossy fruitwood. Design: Carlos Alberto Cruz; Photo: Stan Rumbough

Startling crimson-clad regimental guards flank the stone-paved approach to a tropical transit porch. A jungle-like clutter of plants and frogs is fearlessly mixed and matched without respect for materials, periods, or places of origin. Design: Tony Duquette; Photo: Tim Street-Porter

The entrance should be inviting, pique curiosity, and be amusing to walk through. In this spontaneously casual island house, converted from a chicken coop, time-worn memorabilia, casually stacked bookcases, and a friendly old round table gladden the spirit of all who enter. Design: Loren Dunlap; Photo: Stan Rumbough

Setting the stage for the Victorian eclecticism of this country house, the entry holds a minimum of nearly necessary ingredients: a chair with a decidedly neo-Gothic personality and a container of magical beasts for umbrellas and sunhats. The wallpaper and window treatment echo the charm of a nineteenth-century English cottage. Design: Mark Hampton; Photo: Stan Rumbough

A cross-cultural vestibule leading to the kitchen and paved with Vietnamese baskets provides a bed niche for the family dog under a cushion-covered bench, part of the ministorage wood unit that holds placemats and kitchen and dining linens. Design: Jane Victor & Jennifer Ellenberg; Photo: Norman McGrath

With the secret knowledge that modest things can be more beautiful than anything expensive and that reemphasized period structural details can be part of an entry's purely personal gesture, here, a single Queen Anne–style country chair, a framed biblical print, and a braided rag rug impart an air of serenity and gain contemporary appreciation from the russet-painted divided wall. Design: David Wiggins; Photo: Rob Karosis

Bright, alluring color and the luscious textures of reed, bamboo, rattan, wood, and tile—all crafted by time, weather, and diligent human hands—capture the faraway feel, the magic and lassitude of this Balinese passageway into a house where the verdant tropics invade the rooms throughout. Design: Made Wijaya; Photo: Tim Street-Porter

Crystal and clever lighting transform this windowless entrance of ivory walls and gray carpets into a subtly glowing and highly convivial cocktail room. Guests can admire a beautiful collection of 1930s glass figurines, bookends, paperweights, decanters, and stemware contrasted by leatherbound volumes of nineteenth-century greats such as Balzac and Stendhal, all gathered from French antique shops and Parisian flea markets. Design: Odette Boulenger for Lalique; Photo: Tim Ebert

When the prelude to a home is an exalting crescendo of beautifully
formed stairs, little else is needed. Still, there's room for individualistic
expression. The expected: elegant linen-white paint. The unexpected:
a thin, tall, mini-monument to an angel. Design: Cameron, Cameron &
Taylor; Photo: Peter Peirce

The entrance hall: a hyphen between the exterior and interior worlds.
The banisters and stairs: parentheses in time and space. Here they
provide a glowing embrace for all who are welcomed into this elegantly
decorated realm of eclectically assembled golden treasures.
Design: Jamie Drake; Photo: Peter Peirce

A golden fantasy tree branches out to connect painterly whimsy with bare-boned architectural ingenuity to transform this standard apartment foyer into one of fairy-tale enchantment. The circular burst of tiles and plump pumpkins on the floor inspire entrants to follow the yellow brick road. Design: Dominique Lange and Lisa Wassong; Photo: Michael Slack

A single family heirloom—an antique country armoire—asserts its worthy presence amid the powerful scale and geometry of this light-flooded entryway that interprets the massive overhead beams of colonial Mexico in a thoroughly contemporary way. Design: Manolo Mestre; Photo: Tim Street-Porter

A sweeping modern grand entrance in the
Bauhaus idiom centers around its lofty geometry.
The dramatic space overlooking the dunes fea-
tures an eclectic handful of favorite things,
including a sprouting scallion sculpture, an
Art Deco chair, and a Japanese chest.
Design: Robert Madey; Photo: Bill Rothschild

In a Rocky Mountain ski retreat, the stairway
near the entry point sets the tone for a house in
close communication with its forest surroundings
and panoramic views of snowy peaks. The
wrought-iron banister imitates twigs and, along
with the huge, rotund Native American pottery,
gives a preview of the rest of the rustic eclectic
furnishings. Design: Juan Pablo Molyneux;
Photo: Billy Cunningham

Urbane and polished, this windowless apartment entrance draws its swash-buckling architectural confidence from historically inspired zebra-style laid marble floors and rich koa paneling. The spectacular walls serve as a gallery backdrop for photographs by Stieglitz and a prized Rodin sculpture.
Design: Juan Pablo Molyneux; Photo: Billy Cunningham

As the entrance corridor narrows and takes a turn, the stunning floor treat-ment imparts continuity to the space while the gallery aura gives way to a trio of customary entrance features: a handsome mirror, a place for keys and mail, an attractive container for fresh flowers. Design: Juan Pablo Molyneux; Photo: Billy Cunningham

Eclecticism builds upward from vestibule floor to second- and third-story stairways in an 1890s townhouse restored with a contemporary sensibility. The original adventurous architect was already mixing French parquets with English and Japanese woodwork and burgeoning influences from the Arts and Crafts movement. Design: Marcy Balk; Photo: Peter Peirce

The foyer as the central artery of a luxurious apartment, perhaps a waiting room, elicits several traditional first-impression components, including a series of eclectically mixed friezes and sconces building up toward an entrance classic—a prized medieval tapestry. Design: Robert de Carlo, courtesy of American Hospital of Paris French Designer Showhouse; Photo: Phillip H. Ennis

An Arabian night's spectacle on the California oceanfront is actually a tricultural journey from point one, an Italian-style stone-bench terrace, to point two, a French neoclassical staircase, from where this view was taken, through walls richly ornamented with damascene panels and inlaid Syrian chairs. Design: Juan Pablo Molyneux; Photo: Charles S. White

Guests are met by a magical jewel-like intimacy in this emerald-green vestibule, where the heavily textured two-tone paint enhances the ornamental nature of the quirky international furnishings, dominated by the gilt and sparkle, the paisleys and tigers, of India. Design: Roberto Bergero; Photo: Erica Lennard

As culturally astute as its well-traveled owners, this spacious, tranquil entrance hall proves the connection between the primitive and the refined as it combines Nepalese masks, Buddhist tonkas, and Asian iconography with Early American furniture and German Expressionist paintings. Design: Courtesy of Arts & Antiques magazine; Photo: Bill Rothschild

Under the principal staircase, the formal entrance hall forbids familiarity and inexorably urges and ushers flow into the main social areas through its sweeping checkerboard floor. Its ingredients classically, properly belong here— the upright silken chairs, the towering antique clock, the Regency candelabras and rose-filled vases, the console with mirror. Design: Raphael Serrano, courtesy The Royal Oak Foundation; Photo: Fernando Bengoechea

A lovely white American Victorian staircase sets off a dazzling array of exotica from Victorian India. Among these fabulous items: a carved maharajah's table with a silver base, a mother-of-pearl inlaid chest, a lighting fixture featuring fretwork characteristic of the Raj, framed prints of Nepalese birds, and a colossal conch shell found on the wilder shores of the Indian Ocean. Design: Tom Britt; Photo: Bill Rothschild

Once in a while an entry leads almost immediately into the living room. In this resplendent New York apartment, the exquisite marquetry floor helps guide visitors in and a stylish Russian Empire jardiniere, prominently placed against the back of the sofa, identifies where one space ends and another begins. Design: Juan Pablo Molyneux; Photo: Billy Cunningham

Entrances
details

One's arrival in the eclectic home is greeted by marvelous objects foreshadowing a voyage of discovery. A signature piece or grouping instantly reveals personality. Whether it features an heirloom console, a Scandinavian grandfather clock, a tribal totem, a gallery-style lineup of contemporary art, or—more formally—an embossed leather chair and tapestry, the entry should express both friendliness and flow.

Animal Shelter

The vestibule can be a great sleep space for the family dog. Here, under a complex mini-storage unit embellished with Southeast Asian baskets, a cushion-covered bench shelters the pet's bed niche.

Rustic Romance

Pure lines exude authentic welcome and give off a sense of spiritual comfort. The functional form of a solitary chair—a practical repository for things brought in from the outside—proves that style resides as much in the modest as in the extravagant entryway.

Setting the Stage

Rather than a traditional chandelier in the entrance, an unusual lantern or an exotically ornate lighting fixture, such as this from the time of the Raj, brings India's Victoriana into an American Victorian entry and immediately establishes the eclectic ambience of the home.

Birds of a Feather

Pleasant collectibles—such as botanical prints, bird paintings, and dog pictures—rather than family photographs, crowded gallery-fashion and lining a stair wall in similar frames, tend to create the ambience but not too much intimacy in what is basically a space for moving on rather than lingering.

Umbrellas, Etc.

Perhaps one necessary feature of an entrance or foyer is a container of bamboo or porcelain, tole or marble, for umbrellas and walking sticks. In the eclectic style, the more unusual the container, the better. Here, a pair of fantasy beasts adds a distinctive touch.

Tropical Welcome

Steps are bound to quicken and expectations rise when an extraordinary find, such as these colorful regimental guards, greets visitors to a home. The tropical transit porch of this eclectic house promises many more surprises.

Sense of Place

The twig banister of wrought iron in this Rocky Mountain house in the woods illustrates how the entry hall can connect the eclectic interior with its outside surroundings. At the same time, such a feature is a prelude to the decor awaiting inside.

Passage to India

A small city apartment contains the most exotic passageway, adorned with a treasure trove of bright Indian objects. Dark, deeply brilliant, and textured application of paint on the walls emphasizes an aura of jewel-box richness and coziness.

Formal Introduction

Along the principal staircase of a formal reception hall, certain elements make the grand statement appropriate to such architectural spaciousness. Pale-hued walls, patterned marble floors, and a prominently placed long-case antique clock are among its ideal adornments.

City Attractions

A customary ingredient of city apartment entryways is a mirror—an ornate gilded Chippendale, one with a Chinese lacquer frame, or a simple watered version—whose function is to give the illusion of more space. Also typical: a place for keys and a mail tray, as well as a wonderful container for a bouquet of fresh flowers or a splendid potted plant.

Tapestries in Transit

As in traditional decor, the eclectic hallway—especially if it boasts a lofty ceiling—is the natural place for hanging an impressive vertical tapestry. Be it a precious heirloom from Renaissance Flanders or a modern macramé hanging, a single large pictorial piece can bring warmth and animation to an awkward, undefined space.

Eclectic Living Rooms

If the living room has everything to do with how life is lived or how space is made to accommo-date the many ways individuals choose to occupy it, then it is eclecticism that is necessary to make this space home. For today, existence itself is eclectic.

Images of rocket ships and kinti cloths, the music of Palestrina intertwined with throbbing techo sounds are part of every day. Such extra-ordinary sensory juxtaposi-tions influence our notions of comfort, hospitality, and style. They affect how we carry forward fan-ciful objects from bygone eras into our own high-velocity age. For whether it's serene or hip, mono-chromatically neutral or bombarded with color, the eclectic living room is a product of its time. Its domestic aesthetic is never far removed from the pulse of the larger universe outside.

For example, once upon a time every home had both a front parlor and a back parlor. One was an off-limits drawing room reserved for entertaining. The other was a sitting room where family mem-bers gathered for music, reading, and conversation. Nowadays the rule is that if the living room is comfortable for forty, then it should be comfort-able for four—or one. With space at a premium, we relish the innovative, multipurpose use we can make of a room designed for "living."

Still, this is the most public space inside. Perhaps influenced by trendy loft arrangements, which are particularly suited to the eclectic style, we tend to favor living rooms that are divided into several intimate zones. Here, clusters of furniture—

anchored by area rugs, architectural distinctions, or ingenious use of paint—fulfill specific func-tions. Conversational groupings might center around the hearth, under an important painting or a glorious view. One corner might serve as a library-study-office. Another could revolve around a gaming-table and also be a spot for taking tea. Ideally, a carefully choreographed spatial flow facilitates these groupings. Comfortable arm-chairs, whimsical stools, occasional tables, ottomans, and chests placed in close proximity make talk easy. Unique period sofas, sinuous chaise longues, pillow-covered French country benches, a baby grand piano or a harp, unusual surfaces for drinks and finger food, novel forms of lighting provide eclectic departure points. So do tactile heirlooms, fluffy or silky throws, and myriad intriguing personal mementos.

A successful eclectic living room conveys a strong sense of choices made, values embraced. Its sum clearly expresses what matters to the people at home in it. Because this is a room for sharing, the best and showiest possessions belong here. This is the proper arena for friends to enjoy what the owners believe is good, true, and beautiful. Here's the place to gladden hearts with original art and authentic period furniture, eccentric folkcraft and the finest silver, yards and yards of window fabric astonishingly draped, and precious floor coverings that make each step a pleasure.

Previous pages: Histories fuse in this urbane international living room. From the 1960s comes a transparent chair of Lucite; from the 1940s, a bronze Giacometti coffee table; from the 1930s, an Art Deco portrait by Jean Dupas. Then there's the Mexican "hand" chair by Pedro Friedeberg, some lacquered bamboo from Kyoto, and an antique Waterford crystal chandelier. Design: Larry Laslo; Photo: Stewart O'Shields, from *The Table*, by Diane Von Furstenberg

Bright, Moroccan-style tiles are bathed in sunlight and surrounded by stripes of Napoleonic desert campaigns. They pull around a sophisticated coalition of black-and-white art photographs, a jewel-like Malmaison bird, an ornate eighteenth-century Indian buffet, and Islamic-style mother-of-pearl armchairs cushioned in purple. Design: Denis Colomb; Photo: Erica Lennard

A fireplace that floats in the window, a clutch of Andean silver objects, and a six-part painting from the Cuzco School stir up an international excitement within these fascinatingly conceived walls that bring the outdoors inside the living room. Design: Carlos Alberto Cruz; Photo: Stan Rumbough

Liberally mixing art with furniture that is historically and structurally poles apart leads to dramatic decor and a savvy, international style. Along a wall full of much-used books, Mies van de Rohe's modern chairs have no trouble relating to a seventeenth-century Spanish caballero's ornate writing throne. Design: Carlos Alberto Cruz; Photo: Stan Rumbough

Objects appropriate to their Western ski mountain setting share a visual language, though their backgrounds span the globe. The rug is from India; the coffee table was a Nepalese shutter. The table behind the sofa is Spanish Colonial; the motorized panel that closes off the kitchen is a *trompe l'oeil* Georgia O'Keefe sunflower; the eighteenth-century eagle console was stripped of its gilt and its marble top replaced by a slab of koa. Design: Juan Pablo Molyneux; Photo: Billy Cunningham

In the same living room, the dramatic fireplace, topped by a soaring American eagle, is made of rough pine beams and Arizona stone, with the center section hiding a built-in television–home video unit for viewing after strenuous days of schussing down the ski slopes. Design: Juan Pablo Molyneux; Photo: Billy Cunningham

A monochromatic scheme of ocher, ecru, and honey tones in jute, mohair, polyester, and raw silk gathers tribal momentum through a Dogon ladder and a trapezoid drum from Mali. The room's futuristic edge is sharpened by a cubistic application of paint and such stark geometric forms as the cocktail table of Japanese tamo wood. Design: Jane Victor & Jennifer Ellenberg, courtesy of American Hospital of Paris French Designer Showhouse; Photo: Norman McGrath

Clad in various paisley weaves and the intrinsic charm of its slat floors and wooden beams, this New England living room's collection of objects from China, India, Africa, and America conveys an easy, just-arrived feeling. There is a wonderful spontaneity to the mix—a natural rather than decorated atmosphere. Design: Barbara Colman; Photo: Peter Jaquith

The soul of the American Southwest animates this living room. The focus is on the comforts of an imposing sofa, decked out in an antique serape, behind a wonderfully battered Mexican coffee table with a display of extraordinary local folk art. Design: Martin Kuckly, Kuckly Associates, Inc.; Photo: Peter Vitale

Lighting takes many artful, wild, and eccentric forms in this spacious Maine living room magnetized around a north-country fireplace and an Oushak rug. Its ambience is dedicated to several generations savoring the nearby sea and sylvan surroundings. Design: Martin Kuckly, Kuckly Associates, Inc.; Photo: Story Litchfield

Paint and fabric—a sophisticated palette of grays and golds—holds
together several unusual groupings of furniture in a living room where
the piano and the pursuit of music are very much the focus of both
design and leisure hours. Design: Ann Lenox; Photo: Steve Vierra

An eclectic pick of African, Asian, and modern art invites a palette of pales for this coolly low-key but atmospherically warm and welcoming living room. Seating is arranged precisely around the hearth to make conversation natural and easy. Design: Susan Federman; Photo: David Duncan Livingston

Ingredients expected and unexpected in a living room turn this loft
into a paradigm of eclecticism. It starts with an old, untuned piano,
a stately eighteenth-century mirror, and a Mission sofa. It culminates
with a finial that once was the peak of a building, a bust of the come-
dian Fernandel, and a mountain bike, permanently parked. Design:
Laurence Kriegel; Photo: Fernando Bengoechea

For an inveterate eclectic collector, living in a single room can rise to highly entertaining occasions
with a giddy array of colorful Indian pillows, Directoire-striped curtains, starburst mirrors, and jeweled coronets orbiting a fancy brass daybed. Design: Charles Riley; Photo: Tim Street-Porter

A joyous spontaneity and lived-in feeling ricochets through this living room, which is arranged with a bookish continuity. It serves as a space for reading, contemplation, and conversation around a pony rug and Hepplewhite chairs neatly cushioned and upholstered in Oxford cloth.
Design: Loren Dunlap; Photo: Stan Rumbough

Against a beloved view of modern Boston, meaningful memorabilia such as the antique cigar-store Native American figure and nicely bound volumes gather like old friends to create the feel of a library in this cozy living room. The literary theme is emphasized by wallpaper in the fashion of bookbindings and upholstery in a similar trapunto pattern. Design: Richard Fitzgerald; Photo: Steve Vierra

A melting pot of contemporary informality with a
distinct beat of the global village makes easy
neighbors of handmade rugs and pottery from Mali
and bold curtains of Napoleon III stripes. Denis
Colomb's sleek, vaguely industrial furniture on
wheels invites both relocation and relaxation.
Design: Denis Colomb; Photo: Erica Lennard

For an American photographer who travels around the world, an Argentine decorator living in Paris restored the original mirror and recomposed the architecture of a seventeenth-century space into a living loft. In a quintessential cross-breeding of design cultures, he filled it with antique Rajastani silks, a brilliantly painted screen, a tropical birdcage, an iron Provençal daybed, and an Empire sleigh bed.
Design: Roberto Bergero; Photo: Erica Lennard

Living with contemporary art poses the challenge of making the art friendly to essentially social space. In this light-filled room, integration of the
busy walls into the fabric of life succeeds mostly through the simple
sweep of the furniture and the sophisticated buzz of the floor.
Design: Marshall Watson Interiors Ltd. and Adair Matthews;
Photo: Peter Margonelli

An artist's casually displayed paintings, lining and leaning against the wall, supply the color for this sunny, elongated room. Visitors seated in several groups can chat about their hosts' favorite finds, not least of which is the 1940s lamp on the backgammon table.
Design: Loren Dunlap; Photo: Stan Rumbough

The most treasured, most elaborate, showiest stuff in the
house belongs in the living room. Here, the Far East makes a
civilizing sweep and unites two separate rooms through a
resplendent eighteenth-century Japanese screen and mural-like
Chinese wallpaper. Design: Gold & Genauer Associates
Photo: Bill Rothschild

In the era of the global village, a Western living room turns
into a personalized space for Eastern style spiritual retreat.
Mini-shrines throw light from above on a tea arrangement,
embellished by candles and a colorful kimono that's a regular
part of the decor. Seating, traditionally Japanese, is on the
floor. Design: Yvette Gervey; Photo: Bill Rothschild

A serpentine gilt mirror from the Regency period emphasizes
the creamy, yellowish marble fireplace as the classic gravita-
tional focus of the living room. The subtle sheen of the upholstery, the color cast of the rug, the selections of porcelain on
the mantel all work in tandem to perpetuate a golden aura.
Design: Cullman & Kravis; Photo: Peter Peirce

Edged by woodsy fields and a trompe-l'oeil lake view, this lake-
side living room turns inside out with wicker and twigs, gerani-
ums and garden statuary, Spanish moss and sisal, and a cheery
array of floral prints with roots in Victorian times and the 1950's.
Design: Richard RIdge; Photo: Peter Peirce

Like a dramatist in full command of his singular talents and well versed in the nuanced vocabulary of the twentieth century, the designer of this utterly smooth, worldlywise living room blends a bit of Asia and Egypt with this and that from the 1930s and 1950s to come up with a daringly original realm. Design: Jacques Grange for John Widdicomb Company; Photo: Phillip H. Ennis

This living room is an avant-garde laboratory of taste tinged with love for the colors and forms of the 1940s. Nostalgic mixes with classic and high tech in Olivier Gagnere's angled rug and peekaboo screen, Garouste-Bonetti's tufted red sofa and gold-leaf lamp tree, Martin Szekely's sinuous green velvet sofa and black chaise, and Don Friedman's whimsical techno-creature stool, called **Zoidette.** Design: Gerard Dalmon of Neotu Gallery; Photo: Erica Lennard

Neither the priceless antiquities inside, nor the breathtaking Rocky Mountain scenery outside are permitted to overtake the elegant ease of this living room. Discretely distributed Greco-Roman marble heads and Cycladic and Egyptian treasures are organically at one with the Peking-brown Saladino sofa and Pyrex lamp as well as the casual cashmere throws and wicker chairs. Design: John F. Saladino; Photo: William Waldron

Peking brown and jade green provide a subtle thematic and color link to the other side of this splendid living room where its capacious eclecticism absorbs seventeenth-century Japanese screen, an antique Italian chest, a couple of ancient Roman heads, and a 1920 Art Deco chair by Ruhlman. Design: John F. Saladino; Photo: William Waldron

Open to the country air, a pint-size living room
is alive with big ideas. Symmetry and eclecticism
are key to its approachable elegance. A well-fin-
ished floor and beautifully painted ceiling provide
the framework for the amply detailed mirror,
lighting, screen, sofa, and coffee table.
Design: Marshall Watson Interiors Ltd.; Photo:
Keith Scott Morton

Spatial limitations need not hinder eclectic flights
of imagination. Stenciled floors and ceilings pick
up the rhythmic design and superb integration of
plaids and stripes for a total effect of balance,
comfort, wonderful cohesion, and original point
of view. Design: Marshall Watson Interiors Ltd.;
Photo: Keith Scott Morton

A reflection on the past with today's love for fresh color
and clean, unadulterated lines exudes a timelessness
that is also timely. Around a handsome pedimental fireplace
move exquisite cross-currents of Chinese dynastic objects
and furnishings, with English grace notes such as the
blue Morris chairs and the spider-leg occasional tables.
Design: Courtesy *Historic Preservation* magazine; Photo:
David Duncan Livingston

A theatrical fantasy in scarlet merges 1950s Hollywood studio swank with
a symmetric array of Chinese, Mexican, Turkish, and Scandinavian pieces.
These are set around the focal points of a zebra rug and a bamboo boat bed.
Design: Arlene Stone; Photo: David Duncan Livingston

Living Room

details

Comfortable armchairs, a sofa for loung-
ing, atmospheric lights, and surfaces
for books and beverages are living room
essentials. Eclecticism materializes via
an astute mix of star pieces and show-
stopping details. Remember, opposites
attract. Furnishings placed in juxtaposi-
tion gain strength from differences as
well as similarities. Curves and angles
play off each other for ambience. Picture
windows, fireplaces, niches, and lofty
ceilings suggest decorating focal points.

Mirror, Mirror

A beautiful mirror has enormous power to civilize
the aura of a living room, to create the illusion of
space, and to animate other furnishings with
unexpected reflection and sparkle.

Exotic Grouping

The lavish amber adornments of an extraordinary
eighteenth-century turquoise buffet from India
interact with the hues of Moroccan tiles and
Napoleonic desert stripes. The campaign fabric,
the antique Bonaparte chair, and Empress
Josephine's jeweled Malmaison bird bear
thematic affinity, as do the French art photos
taken around the Taj Mahal. Design: Denis
Colomb; Photo: Erica Lennard

Surface Synergy

A little round table with an hourglass base,
hinting of nineteenth-century Europe, and a low
hexagonal table inspired by the complex designs
of Asia are among the types of occasional tables
that provide plenty of contrast as well as surfaces
on which to put things. Design: Jacques Grange
Collection at Beacon Hill Showrooms; Photo:
Phillip H. Ennis, courtesy of John Widdicomb
Company

All in the Game

Gaming tables hark back to a calmer time when
family togetherness meant whiling away the
evening with board games, card games, chess,
or backgammon. Leather-wrapped card tables
and antique American tea tables add charm and
create their own intimate corners in the eclectic
living room.

Connective Tissue

Because the floor represents the largest canvas in the living room, it may be the best place to begin a decorating scheme. Division of the room into separate groupings can be established through area rugs or a single floor covering that helps merge everything into a coherent unit.

Let There Be Light

Among the most stunning eclectic effects in the living room are born of interesting indirect lighting. Sleek 1930s torchères, classic papery Noguchi lamps, witty 1950s sconces—all make individualistic statements. A few are delightfully unabashed scene-stealers, such as this gold-leaf tree lamp, which is as much sculpture as illuminator.

The Perfect Chair

A glamorous wood-framed, neutral-hued salon chair, upholstered in velvet and reminiscent of the 1930s, embodies the spirit of comfort and versatility, looking backward and looking forward, which is the signature of the eclectic living room. It would mix as well with Burmese water jars as with Chinese wedding chests, a Renaissance tapestry, or a Rauschenberg collage. Design: Jacques Grange Collection at Beacon Hill Showrooms; Photo: Phillip H. Ennis, courtesy of John Widdicomb Company

Mini Merger

As new as it is old, this tribal-style stool with its classic aerodynamics is the kind of piece that suits the playful mergers-and-acquisitions aesthetic associated with eclectic living room vignettes. Its slight hint of Egypt makes it as compatible with Art Deco as with pristine Japanese screens or opulently gilded Empire artifacts and rich French silks. Design: Jacques Grange Collection at Beacon Hill Showrooms; Photo: Phillip H. Ennis, courtesy of John Widdicomb Company

Personal Grouping

An artist's personal motto suggests this appealingly self-expressive and artfully artless arrangement in one corner of the living room. The roses in the sconce connect with the roses on one stool, which relates in turn to the needlepoint texture of the charmingly mismatched second stool. Design: Loren Dunlap; Photo: Stan Rumbough

Eclectic
Dining Areas

Where we break bread together and raise our glasses in happy unison, the most generously sociable and communal spot in the home has become an eclectic paradox. To a large extent, tradition still holds court in the dining room.

It is replete with memories of aroma-stimulated appetites, scintillating good talk, candlelit romantic intimacy, multicourse holiday meals, and special occasions reuniting far-flung families. Yet iconoclastic forces of recent times—which have reordered the way we live—have virtually redefined the dining space. The strictly designated formal dining room, left silent and empty a great deal of the time, still exists. But the site of eating and entertaining these days has become much more flexible. It can be a screen-partitioned area in an artist's loft or a convivial corner of an apartment; a cozy breakfast nook or a book-lined double-duty room where work and study alternate with dining and celebrating.

No matter how big or where it is, today's shared table shapes up with certain eclectic ingredients and novel forms. Just as such once-exotic flavors as lemon grass, octopus, passion fruit, and tamarind now star in home-composed menus, unexpected mergers of East and West, hot and cool, rough and smooth, applied to the decorative brew of the dining room can animate the senses and awaken the spirit of a place. The dining area is the perfect platform for cleverly crossbred furnishings and tabletop designs. It is also a natural stage where the personal style of the host or hostess can publicly shine.

The eclectic dining room is a dynamic place. The energy in the room emanates not only from the chemical reaction between people but also from the special frisson that comes from unorthodox combinations. Though the room's

essentials have hardly changed over the centuries—a solid surface for eating surrounded by a seating arrangement, with a nearby sideboard, console, or other handy server—the international style and carefree mixed-period manner in which these ingredients are assembled has dramatically transformed dining ambience. Chairs no longer need to match, for instance. Some of the most diverting and distinct dining aggregates these days feature half a dozen chairs from just as many artisan eras, casually juxtaposing a mid-twentieth-century tubular steel and leather design with a clean-lined wooden country chair or provocatively placing a spindly contemporary black iron chair next to a phantasmagorically carved Gothic number.

The simplicity of the Japanese way of dining has had a major influence on eclectic pairings. Translucent shoji screens have a marked affinity for American industrial furniture and high-tech lamps from Italy. Screens, be they as elaborate as a coromandel or simply some beautiful fabric tacked on to three panels, along with wall detailing such as moldings, wood paneling, murals, wallpapers, and stenciling, add sensory richness and emotional comfort to a dining arrangement. Chandeliers, indirect lighting, silver candlesticks, and side lighting from unique sconces and torchères add glamour and glow. Finally, as informality continues to replace stuffiness and protocol and barriers between dining rooms and other rooms break down, sari cloths and Balinese batiks, Guatemalan weaves, heirloom Bessarabian rugs, or brand-new dhurrie rugs all can be used imaginatively to delineate the borders of the ever-evolving dining sphere.

Previous pages: Lofty greenery
outside raised ranch windows
and high-beamed architecture are
welcomed into this elegant country
dining room. A serenade in blue is
played by decorative instruments
of international origin. Portuguese
tile keys the mirror and combination
console and wine rack. Rows of
blue-and-white china top the beam
and dictate the pattern of the chair
upholstery around the Chinese
Chippendale table. Design: David
Barrett; Photo: Bill Rothschild

A collector can encrust a dining room with history. Here a museum's worth of splendors—energized
by flower and fruit arrangements on Napoleonic epergnes—makes dining an imperial experience.
The glass-topped Art Deco table by Randt mirrors Napoleon's sister's flatware; the chairs were
made for Josephine and the furniture and cherished objects are replete with references to the
Bonaparte era. Design: Roger Prigent, Malmaison Antiques; Photo: Stewart O'Shields, from *The
Table*, by Diane Von Furstenberg

A deliciously eccentric dove-footed Regency Italian side table flanked by Georgian armchairs is the cynosure of a five-sided transitional space. For convenience and because its buttery walls, jaunty French barometer, and bouquet-shaped candle shields engender intimacy, the owners use it more often than the designated dining room—a froth of green and white fabric around a Danish Bornholm clock, seen in the background. Design: Lise Davis at James Billings Antiques and Interiors; Photo: Peter Jaquith

Le style français is a perpetual laboratory of taste. This pastel-pretty Parisian dining room, with its deft combination of disparate objects, acknowledges with insight the hold of a delicately gilded architectural past over the outrageous design whimsies of the present. Design: Roberto Bergero; Photo: Erica Lennard

Pushing the newest fibers, materials, and textures unexpectedly into a classical symmetrical framework, this tailored dining area closely relates to the living room of which it is an integral part by a repetition of rectangular forms and a respectful but witty adherence to traditionalism with a twist. Design: Marshall Watson Interiors Ltd.; Photo: Mick Hales

A prized possession—an octet of startling black Burmese chairs—suggests this center-stage circular dining room display, where impact is squared and heightened by the elaborate architectural effects of the mirrored, coffered ceiling hung with a resplendent chandelier.
Design: Hagman & Yaw Architects, Ltd.; Photo: Dave Marlow/Aspen

Bold colors set the stage for buffet entertaining. Note the underlying restraint of related round shapes—classic and novel—and how the essence of dissimilar materials—glass table, Fiestaware ceramics, the marble and velvet—all shine through. Design: Marshall Watson Interiors Ltd. and Adair Matthews; Photo: Peter Margonelli

Empires are at peace here as an eighteenth-century French banquette and four Russian Empire chairs mingle around a dining table covered with luxurious fabrics and sparkling with crystal. The 1930s lamps, side table, and painting as well as the faux-Imperial marbleized strips and cast-iron tacks on the wall and on the gilt-sprinkled floors complete the aura of olden, golden, comfortable grandeur. Design: Odile de Schietere; Photo: Erica Lennard

Rarefied and restrained components of an eclectic assemblage of European furnishings and table garniture are culled from several countries and centuries. Together they make dining in the presence of an original Matisse drawing stand out as a truly golden experience. Design: Adrienne Vittadini and Pigi Carotti; Photo: Peter Peirce

When Art Nouveau fuses with Art Deco and the dining room becomes a glowing gallery of period furnishings, a muted, "undecorated" backdrop works best. This rare 1905 Louis Majorelle dining set, the Tiffany torchère of favrile glass, and the Viennese Müller Brothers chandelier are set off by demitone walls and a Tabriz rug. The sole color departure is a 1940 Hans Hofmann painting. Design: Ellen Goldstein Interiors; Photo: Bill Rothschild

Screens can create festive intimacy. A champagne-and-caviar mood fizzes
in this worldly room of lacquered Biedermeier chairs, German Romantic
period sculptures, and silvered, gilt Viennese fin de siècle artifacts.
The 1950s screen depicts a confetti fantasy of Manhattan skyscrapers.
A stunning centerpiece of carved Macassar ebony holds a crush of
flowers, candles, and black velvet butterflies. Design: Jamie Drake;
Photo: Peter Peirce

Luscious pastel walls blend and emphasize artistic and architectural differences of centuries and create an appealing spatial tension between the sleek, streamlined steel-and-leather modern dining arrangement and the precious antique Chinese console below a prized painting. The cool gleam of exquisitely crafted silver objects, strategically placed here and there, also helps integrate vastly unrelated elements. Design: Ben Baxt; Photo: Peter Peirce

A refreshing breeze of eclecticism riffles through this 150-year-old country dining room with airy Roman curtains draped over its uneven windows and Hepplewhite shield-back chairs (1920s version) painted mint green. The chairs' pleasing Prince-of-Wales feathers are reflected in the lines of the eighteenth-century French landscape gardening plans framed against the creamy wall. Design: Debra A. Blair; Photo: Peter Peirce

International style and improvisational dash seductively blur the spheres of eating and entertaining in this sophisticated yet informal black-and-white country room. The space is dominated by a pair of Directoire daybeds and full of surprisingly placed Chinese, English, and French furnishings and accents. Design: Virginia Witbeck; Photo: Erica Lennard

Retro meets techno as this antique, masculine pedestal table is squared between two stark, sleek modern chairs standing on the clean lines of their wire legs. The small dining area, both urban and urbane, is unexpectedly unified by a diamond-patterned screen and brown-and-white plaid curtains. Design: David Scott; Photo: Peter Peirce

The restrictions of space inspire this buoyant, welcoming corner for dining solo or tea for two. A room that is all things—including sleep space—derives its sunny, airy feeling from blue-and-yellow balloon shades that match the bedspread and wallpaper and a pair of colorfully painted balloon-back chairs placed around a tiny, round wrought-iron table. Design: Michael Love, Interior Options; Photo: Bill Rothschild

Rough Colorado limestone walls in the Frank Lloyd Wright idiom
share their strong personality with an equally eloquent collection
of antiques from the East and antiquities from the West. An Archaic
head of a goddess and an ancient Greek sculpted bull's head
bond around the dining table with an eighteenth century kimono,
a lacquered Japanese trunk, and a Chinese temple dog. Design:
John F. Saladino; Photo: William Waldron

In the same dining room, a sixteenth-century Japanese sculpture of a monk hovers along
bookshelves whose squares enshrine a prized collection of antiquities: Cycladic idols, a
Greco-Roman head, Attic vessels, and a seated Egyptian figure. Design: John F. Saladino;
Photo: William Waldron

In a breathtaking merger of aesthetics, Middle Eastern ornamentation meets European elegance. A carved, inlaid, gilded seventeenth-century niche from Damascus, damascene amber prayer beads, filigreed silver, and densely woven, highly patterned silk are at once toned down and played up by a lovely French table, discreet Swedish chairs (both nineteenth century), the finely detailed neoclassical palmetto crown molding, and the delicate smocking on the curtains. Design: Juan Pablo Molyneux; Photo: Charles S. White

Chinese zodiac figures and the mannered architecture of a landmark Federal house dictate a formal but lighthearted tone and influence the blue-and-white palette of the toile-de-Jouy fabric on the windows and walls—the chinoiserie weave in the brand-new carpet as well. Victorian chairs surround a nineteenth-century New York table, where the color scheme continues through napery, stemware, and china.
Design: Juan Pablo Molyneux; Photo: Billy Cunningham

Dinner in toyland: Checks and plaids, candy-striped wallpaper, myriad old-fashioned playthings, and merrily painted furnishings are brought to the nth degree of creativity. Colorful seedbags are sewn into slipcovers for the children's chairs and six entirely different 1940s tablecloths fashioned into absolutely enchanting storybook curtains. Design: Ann Fox, Room Services; Photo: Bill Rothschild

An almost giddily romantic atmosphere emanates from an uninhibited
mix of antique crystal, gilt, wrought-iron Spanish, Chinese, and
French chandeliers, girandoles, candelabras, votive candles, lanterns,
and table lamps that sprout, tower, cascade, dribble, twinkle, and
throw via candlepower a luminous intensity on a dining room of
warm, vivid reds and rosy browns left open to the thick scents
and sounds of the tropical evening. Design: Annie Kelly; Photo: Tim
Street-Porter

East meets West with an experiment in color relationships in a room full
of clutter, memory, and sensuality. A trompe l'oeil mosaic at the threshold sets the tone for the wild array of fabrics, artifacts, maps, prints,
lamps, mirrors, and vases bought on meanderings across Europe and
wanderings through the Indian subcontinent. Design: Roberto Bergero;
Photo: Erica Lennard

A multiplicity of worlds merges in this highly personalized dining setup where barriers between rooms dissolve and Victorian toys, miniature Russian onion domes, and piles of books, boxes, and ornamental balls all play together for a comfortable, lived-in effect. Design: Loren Dunlap; Photo: Stan Rumbough

This massive weathered table and the comfortably mismatched chairs—in an artist's country studio, converted from a chicken coop—suggest uses other than dining. A glass jar of sunflowers and bowls of fruit lead the eye to the only fanciful piece in the space: a timeworn sideboard that breaks the stark rectangular lines with Art Nouveau curves. Design: Loren Dunlap; Photo: Stan Rumbough

A wild animal kingdom unexpectedly inhabits this sumptuous dining room furnished with luxuries of many cultures and periods. Deep vermilion walls, color-
cued to the Herend porcelain on the table, elegantly embrace the ferocious
feline plate collection and the mighty elephants, playful monkeys, and spotted
leopards cavorting on the tree-of-life curtain and bamboo chandelier shades
and peering from curtain rods, mantelpieces, and paintings. Design: Diane
Knight Interiors; Photo: Bill Rothschild

The true West echoes in this eclectic Rocky Mountain dining room through
rustic materials and primitive patterns such as a grain-painted blanket chest,
Native American baskets, a kilim rug, and a Georgia O'Keeffe painting. The
foreign note comes from another snow country: alpine terrace chairs adapted
for dining by David Linley, who was inspired at an early Austrian ski resort.
Design: Juan Pablo Molyneux; Photo: Billy Cunningham

In the summer, the dining room may move outside and become an intimate theater for festive al fresco repasts. This traditional all-American terrace is transformed by seductive harem-style use of innocent fabrics, a scattering of mischievous and mysterious Oriental cupids, and well-placed votive candles into a stage for romance. Design: Eugénie Kim; Photo: Bill Rothschild

The offbeat looks of the twentieth century assert themselves in a
sophisticated and almost over-the-top parade through a thouroughly
original dining room. The orange-and-green color combination popu-
lar in the 1950s irreverently pulls together the eclectic mix of chairs,
table, and server. Each piece of furniture and light fixture makes its
own statement about design motifs from the 1930s to the 1990s.
Design: Gerard Dalmon for Neotu Gallery; Photo: Erica Lennard

Inviting in the priceless seascape of an island
morning, this charming breakfast room, with
its open feeling and low-maintenance decor,
radiates its affinity for salt air and blooming
nature. Splashes of cheery prints, a paradisaical
painting, and trompe-l'oeil caprices such as the
topiary étagère in the corner and the painted
plywood window swags all play up the view.
Design: David Barrett; Photo: Bill Rothschild

Piece by Piece Dining Room
details

Perfectly matching dining room sets and table settings are not in the eclectic idiom. Unmatched china or single-style ceramics in several colors yield terrific effects. French or Irish crystal, Belgian linen, and classic European porcelain can frolic with miniature Kenyan soapstone menageries, Chinese toy birds, or Vietnamese reed mats. Opulent antiques look great contrasted with country limestone floors, tatami mats, or exotic sari tablecloths. Affordable textiles and centerpieces of cork, driftwood, or seashells demolish fusty rules and elevate conversation.

Establishing Shot
A single arresting large painting establishes the wild kingdom theme of this opulently furnished, antique- and exotica-filled dining room. The lovely warm vermilion walls also help create cohesion. Design: Diane Knight Interiors; Photo: Bill Rothschild

Romancing Indochine
Dining room sconces made of Southeast Asian cork, wall color paint mixed from banana leaves and green curry, reed mats and chopsticks made in a Vietnamese village are freely mixed with fine Belgian linen placemats, Baccarat stemware, Limoges porcelain plates.
Design: Jane Victor & Jennifer Ellenberg; Photo: Norman McGrath

Mood Makers
Though the dining table and chairs are the focal point of the dining room, splurging on one or more treasures can really exalt the pleasure of entertaining in a splendorous setting. Conversation pieces such as this exquisitely filigreed Venetian lantern and sumptuous Belgian tapestry convey eclectic elegance and power the festive interaction of a successful dinner party. Design: Kenneth Hockin; Photo: Peter Peirce

Safari Sightings
Pulling furnishings and objects from many arts and crafts and furniture periods can effectively underline a wonderful dramatic theme. Here, spotted and other wild and mild animals appear everywhere—on the curtain fabric, the curtain rod, the tabletop, the window sill, and the Chinese console. Design: Diane Knight Interiors; Photo: Bill Rothshcild

International Haute Mix
The atmospheric luxury and personal signature of this table setting is built through the subtle interaction of the muted hues of the Chinese earthenware bowls and the tapestry swirls of the Swedish chair upholstery. Low light from votive candles, individual flower arrangements, the matte sheen of pewter salt and pepper shakers next to each place setting underline the look of caring and meticulously thought-out stylish hospitality.
Design: Juan Pablo Molyneux; Photo: Billy Cunningham

Wonderful Wall Texture

A big gilded mirror with spare, simple, elegant lines and a splendid Empire-style ebonized console with a slender, smallish scale do not overwhelm this relaxing double-duty dining room. Instead, they work in partnership with the unassuming painted wooden walls to pull together such personal effects as the brass-hung reading materials, the paintings, and the collection of plates, silver, and serving accessories of a buffet dinner. Design: Brett Nestler; Photo: Bill Rothschild

Collector's Corner

The dining room is the place for collections on display. Here, against the deep, rich, polished dark wood of a cozy Early American–style sideboard, a glorious gathering of blue-and-white porcelain—something no dining room can ever have too much of—and a whimsical lineup of canine figurines—mostly pugs—lend resonance. Design: Josef Pricci Interiors Photo: Bill Rothschild

Screen Play

As dining room walls dissolve and hierarchical rituals are increasingly replaced by casual accessories that make adventuresome and imaginative use of the zone around even the most glamorously set tables, screens take on bigger roles. Here, an artistically executed, gold-stenciled homemade velvet screen, though dignified, with its medieval lines, brings warmth to the serious antiques in the room. Design: Odile de Schietere; Photo: Erica Lennard

Eclectic Kitchens

Though no one wants to get stuck there, the kitchen is increasingly a magnet. Both old-fashioned sweet spot and high-tech power center of domestic life, today's kitchen—in country or city, in image and reality—tends to be an eclectic place.

Surprisingly, the contemporary kitchen's newly colorful personality and easy elegance may have been triggered by the availability of ever more enabling home technology. Though one might expect digital appliances, cutting-edge gadgets, and programmed equipment to dehumanize the kitchen, just the opposite has occurred. Standardized kitchens are on the wane. Now that the kitchen tends to be the most often updated and remodeled part of the home, it is also the most personalized.

Increasingly tailored to the needs of individual households, the kitchen is becoming much more variable. It is assuming new shapes, new roles. It can be a narrow gourmet galley. Equipped with such cross-cultural extras as a Chinese steamer or a cappuccino maker, the eclectic kitchen is a satisfying nightly craft shop—a creative counterpoint to the office day. More often, the kitchen is an enlarged, organic social center. Wonderful aromas oozing out of bubbling stove and sizzling oven engulf attractively surfaced work areas where family members and good friends pull up a stool, lend a hand, and swap tales with the cook about the day's events.

With its sphere of emotional experiences expanded, today's kitchen embraces an unex-

pected, sometimes contradictory mix of decorative and utilitarian furnishings. Newly invited fineries such as Danish antique armoires and Art Deco consoles, Japanese window treatments and Chinese light fixtures, now look quite at home doing everyday duty. Some new kitchens exude an almost old-time feeling of bounty and warmth with shelves of cookbooks, openly stacked plates, hanging pots, farm-style wooden tables laden with bowls of voluptuous vegetables. Others speak their welcome through the homey patois of handcrafted ethnic elements—Asian cooking tools, sunny Portuguese tiles, French racks for drying herbs.

Thus the wisdom of other cultures enters the kitchen. In addition, a multitude of luxurious and innovative surfaces for counters and floors—such as apricot-colored granite and antiqued limestone—along with stunning architectural stunts that allow for wine alcoves or reach in innovative ways for more natural or artificial light redefine the rules for what belongs in the kitchen.

As the vital triangle of work areas—stove, sink, refrigerator—is neatened through built-ins, pull-outs, and exotic dividers, thematically and texturally the kitchen is more and more a part of the flow and design of the rest of the eclectic home.

A treasured family heirloom, a Colonial chandelier of cast-iron and verde glass, updates its charms in the company of fresh French fabrics and wallpaper. The piece is hung above the centered freestanding worktable—which is now, as in early America, the focal point of the kitchen.
Design: Cynthia Clark Interiors; Photo: Rob Karosis

Beaming bright and fresh as a country morning, this
kitchen, full of favorite things, is anything but naive
about the use of pattern against pattern. Checks,
stripes, and flower prints pick up on one another
in several smart details from floor to ceiling.
Design: Ellen Lemer Korney; Photo: Bill Rothschild

The earthy yet ethereal atmosphere of a light-filled Mediterranean kitchen—part Morocco, part South of France—is captured through hand-made cement tiles, some with enchanting bird imagery. The hint of antiquated rustic rituals is offset by up-to-the-minute power appliances.
Design: Martine Murat for Carocim; Photo: Erica Lennard

A frothy, lacy collection of tropical birdcages from India and Panama is set free from context to serve as room dividers. Looking like airy sculptures, they help open a feeling of fresh abundance and space in this small glass-mosaic kitchen.
Design: Martine Murat for Carocim; Photo: Erica Lennard

A sweeping modern open-plan kitchen combines stainless steel, black granite, and cheery cherrywood. Eclectic features include the quirky, personalizing, conversation-piece accessories and relaxing wickerwork pedal stools. Design: Martin Kuckly, Kuckly Associates, Inc.; Photo: Eric Roth

A spiffy triangular modern kitchen, color-cued to the Biedermeier theme
of the house, is ashine with a wealth of storage cabinets in a warm-hued
wood that interplays with black laboratory work surfacing, black and white
tiles, and brightness falling from antique holophane lamps.
Design: Eddie E. Harris, Harris Sanders; Photo: Hall Puckett

A palette of chalky pastels recaptures the simple lines and happy days of 1950s America. Sunny checkerboard floors, mint-and-white checked modular units, and stainless steel appliances carry the retro theme forward.
Design: *Kitchens, Bedrooms, and Bathrooms* magazine;
Photo: Ray Main

In this mountainside retreat, the kitchen becomes the undeniable heart of the house as muscular old barstools, drenched in the deep hues of the masculine fabrics, are drawn up to the fresh bleached pine counter where autumn preserving and lunch making are in full swing.
Design: Mark Epstein; Photo: Peter Peirce

With a sense of memory and a sense of color, Victoriana and bold modern geometry cross in repeated variations of diamond patterns on the rug, curtain, tablecloth, and glass cabinets, unifying a two-part kitchen and making the most of the many well-lit, well-stored objects.
Design: Marilyn H. Rose Interiors; Photo: Bill Rothschild

Rustic riches of bygone times and a flamboyant passion for collecting come alive against a highly patterned background of quite dissimilar fabrics. What pulls all the busy flourishes together is a clean, hand-painted floor that graphically incorporates the kitchen's three main colors and motifs. Design: Rene Fortgang Interiors; Photo: Bill Rothschild

A traditional white column in a non-traditional place makes an eclectic gesture gracious enough to accommodate the latest sink, refrigerator, and copper-hooded stove. In this narrow, shipshape galley of a white-washed, brass-trimmed kitchen, blue and white wallpaper also adds an old-fashioned note.
Design: Mark Epstein; Photo: Peter Peirce

No end to the eclectic embrace of this fanciful and capacious kitchen, which flirts with demure gingham-backed curtains and white-columned Greek Revival conceits. Behind its old-fashioned mien this practical room holds back nothing when it comes to contemporary culinary empowerment. Design: Marilyn H. Rose Interiors; Photo: Bill Rothschild

Soft vanilla-finished maple cabinets and cherrywood floors contrast sharply with crisp checkerboard tiling and clean-edged navy Formica tops. This neatly packed kitchen, centrally located, is open to house traffic all day long. Design: Marshall Watson Interiors Ltd.; Photo: William Stites

Romanesque curves thrown at unexpected intervals make an intense contrast of light and shadow, secret hollows and pleasing shelf space, in this thoroughly modern kitchen. The space boasts the latest in luxuriously polished but highly practical surfacing. Design: Leopoldo Rosati; Photo: Peter Rymwid

Kitchen
details

Raffia and bamboo. Tropical birdcages and Mediterranean tiles. Techno-modern utilities from Germany and England and retro design elements from l950s America and French Colonial Vietnam. The eclectic kitchen is turning tradition upside down by rearticulating what's fit to live together in the most utilized room in the home. No wonder that along with vital considerations of speed, durability, and easy cleaning comes the challenge of synthesizing atmospheric details.

Eyeful Plateful

It would be a shame to hide vibrantly colored, wonderfully crafted faience pieces when they can enhance the decor of the kitchen. In this high-gloss built-in cabinetry, an open holder displays vertically slid plates and adds interest to the wood's monotony.

Custom Splash

Some of the most successful personal notes in the eclectic kitchen are achieved through hand-painted pictorial tiles. Birds of paradise or favorite fruits and flowers, as here, add whimsy and glamour to the glazed surfaces of the backsplash; the nooks and crannies are easy to keep clean.

Bistro Stools

The best seat in the kitchen is sturdy but flexible. It can be easily moved by the cook and by family members and friends who drop in to help with the preparation of the meal.

Terazzo Tiles

The kitchen as a cool blue getaway at the end of the workday begins at floor level. Here, the latest flexible, easy-care kitchen tiles from Italy sport Caribbean-hued flecks and a terracy texture.
Design: Jamie Drake; Photo: Peter Peirce

Vintage Beauty

The intrinsic sensual appeal of fine wines, with their artistic labels, becomes a vital decorative element of an awkward space in a remodeled New York apartment kitchen. The purest, simplest floor-to-ceiling storage, horizontally lining the bottles, brings to the fore their beauty and the anticipation of the pleasure their contents will convey.
Design: Leopoldo Rosati; Photo: Leopoldo Rosati

Back to the Future

Reminiscent of the warm coziness of country kitchens of yore but catering to contemporary practical needs and ambitious international cooking activity, the deep farm-style sink in stainless steel with a long-neck water faucet cleverly integrates into the new kitchen—textured with historical references, yet exotic.

The Enlightening Past

Newly reproduced antique holophane lamps, with their wonderful striated glass and nickel-plated brass frames, turn the light on where it's most needed—on the cooktops and chopping surfaces of the central worktable.

Eclectic Bedrooms

The realm of dreams and daydreams, the bedroom is in every sense a place of escape. Serene retreat or fantastic voyage, here the imagination is nightly recharged. Because an individual heartbeat throbs beyond its threshold, the bedroom, of all the rooms in the home, holds the greatest promise for decorative self-revelation.

The bedroom naturally absorbs memorabilia, secret treasures, and cherished photographs. It may also hold religious artifacts and intriguing ethnic crafts that look wonderful in their native lands but are hard to integrate back home. The bedroom, thriving on personal history, lends itself to the improvisational brio associated with eclectic taste.

Assembling this microcosm eclectically calls for a venturesome spirit involving time travel, tripping across the planet, or a nostalgic pileup of personal effects. The last may be the most difficult, for its success requires an unsentimental, selective attitude. To make unrelated elements work together, to invoke vibrancy, ease, and an atmosphere of allure—that is an achievement.

The bedroom is primarily a sleep space and the domain of love and passion. For children it is a nest within a nest, a playroom where creative disorder and messy mischief is tolerated. Most people spend one third of their lives in bed, but to house a mattress is but one use of the bedroom. These days the space also serves as a home office, an entertainment venue, and a worldwide communications nerve center.

Cultural cross-currents have entered the bedroom in the last decade, redefining the look

and feel of the bed. It has become more open, softer, and more comfortable—in some ways simplified and purer, in others more complex and theatrical. The idea that one can never toss too many pillows on it is relatively new. So is the acceptance of a plain white sheet, wool blanket, or down comforter as a bedcover. Outlooks on coziness and contentment in a nocturnal resting place have been revolutionized. Take such words as *duvet, futon, featherbed, Eurosquare, boudoir roll, throw:* They are now part of the ABC of a proper bed. Colorful crocheted shawls from Belarus and boldly patterned spreads from Pakistan, Afghanistan, Indonesia, Senegal, Morocco, and the Near East cover many a Western bed. Conversely, there is now a fresh ardor outside the United States for such features of the American bed as patchwork quilts and Hudson Bay and Navajo blankets. Meanwhile, the mosquito veilings of British Colonial Africa, imperial campaign beds from Napoleonic France, sleigh beds, daybeds, recamiers, baldachins, four-posters, iron bedstands, brass frames, lacquered Chinese opium beds, and gilded wooden bedboards with Regency animal imagery are being rediscovered and incorporated in modern sleeping quarters.

Occasionally a marvelous fireplace, a dainty writing desk, or a stunning armoire vies with the bed for attention, but, on the whole, the bed and the bedclothes set the tone for this private stage.

Previous p
the woods
cozy log c
and aspen
above the
covered w
swirling wi
of Eastern
Lueders; P

A witty country-in-the-city take on modernism angles the bed for a more adventurous aura and to soften the hard-lined 1940s desk and split-circle ottoman of the same era. Merry summer-hat colors circle on the straw rug and chickens sprint madly across the screen-printed cotton sateen bedspread.

Design: Jeanne-Aelia Desparmet-Hart of JADH; Photo: Erica Lennard

The twain—Western fineries and Eastern objects of comfort and contentment—meet in an exotic Hawaiian boudoir. Wrapped Feng Shui blessings ritually laid out beside a glass of wine on a japanned chest, a rolled futon, tatami mats, a silken kimono, a rare Chinese chess set, and a gilded French Empire armchair represent both good-luck charms and talismans of taste. Design: Eugenie Kim; Photo: Bill Rothschild

A daring modern sensibility with confident disregard for period rules and geographic barriers mediates an eclectic meeting of African art and furnishings and severe, clean 1940s lines. Soothing earth tones of ocher, rust, gray, blue, and olive in genuinely luxurious textures such as diaphanous paisley, pearly leather, geometric damask, and wool satin unite the room. Design: Jeanne-Aelia Desparmet-Hart of JADH; Photo: Erica Lennard

More stars—for twin babies—with moons and rosy dawns and high-perched animal pals to guard against the dark. Stars scattered everywhere pull together a diversity of styles and elements: faux Dutch moldings, origami lamps, antique cribs, and a plethora of patterns. Stars make an adaptable theme for children's rooms, where cribs give way to beds all too soon. Design: Polly Osborne, Osborne Erickson Architects; Photo: Tim Street-Porter

Centuries of Eastern sensuality—so atmospheric and rich one can almost smell sandalwood and patchouli—are diffused through this elegant tropical bedroom filled with sleek, superbly crafted Asian antiques. The whole is dominated by an ornate Balinese bed.
Design: Amir Rabek; Photo: Tim Street-Porter

Old and new, in intriguing contrast, work in tandem to close off the harsh real world—and again invite it in via television—in this exceptional retreat where the loveliest antique bed, with an almost medieval headboard, is dressed in delicate heirloom linen. A cocoon of gossamer gray moiré hangs by industrial wire hooks and four spare stainless-steel posts. Design: Brian Murphy, BAM Design; Photo: Tim Street-Porter

Extensive world travel, sophisticated restraint, and profound understanding of color are characteristics of its inhabitants revealed by this room. These are expressed through recurring touches of a lovely jade green that pulls together walls, bed, windows, and rug and makes a marvelous backdrop for beloved photographs, paintings, and exquisite furniture acquisitions from the Far East. Design: Barbara Colman; Photo: Peter Jaquith

In a fantastic reinterpretation of the olive-green, burnt orange, protoplasmic free forms of the 1950s, a small bedroom becomes a puzzling world where nothing is quite what it seems. The shirt lamp is a witty nod to Duchamp, the melting clock ticks in Dali's time, and the spliced, snake-like pop creature is Larry Gianettino's bizarre photo-painting of a child's toy.

Design: Gerard Dalmon of Neotu Gallery; Photo: Erica Lennard

Noisy goodnight serenade with an eclectic beat: in the company of pop music icons Elvis, Judy, Peggy Lee, and Johnny Ray, under a sheltering palm of gold upon bold stripes. These reverberate with the throb of the desert and are engulfed by a synchronicity of other favorite things. Design: Michael Davis and Andrew Logan; Photo: Tim Street-Porter

An iconoclastic composition reaches across time and geography around a tall, turned Henri III canopy bed from France with a gamut of accessories ranging from the simplest and sleekest to the most intricately nuanced. In the mix: gold-shot sari cloths, ticking-covered pillows, a Turkish kilim rug, and Denis Colomb's contemporary metal night table on wheels. Design: Denis Colomb; Photo: Erica Lennard

Centuries-old treasures from Italy and South America—some with religious overtones, others bearing the gloss of out-and-out opulence—are crisply, cleanly ordered with an eclectic sensibility. The upholstered walls, ten tailored pillows, beamed brick ceilings, pillars of fieldstone, and unusual shades of paint join in the rich effect. Design: Carlos Alberto Cruz; Photo: Stan Rumbough

The telling yet enigmatic elements that shape a unique life mark the textures of this astonishing bedroom of carmine red. Walls are sponged. The bed is draped with a Turkish cloth. The floor is covered by a bold dhurrie rug. An ancient religious painting, mystical artisanal objects, and favorite photographs are lit by gleams of gold and glints of ornate silver. Design: Larry Totah Design; Photo: Tim Street-Porter

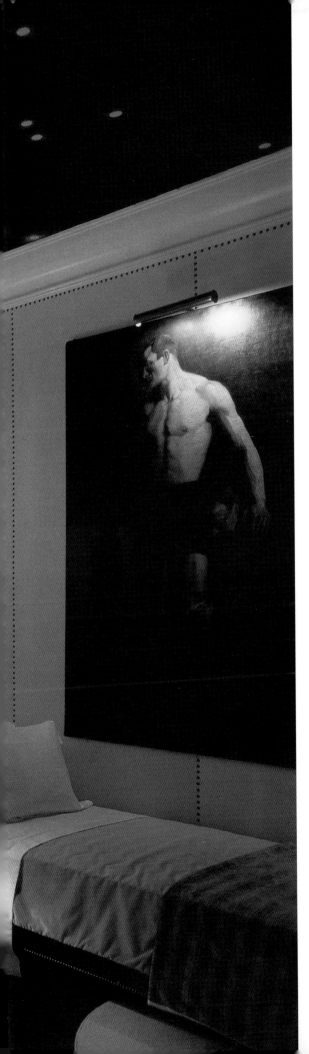

In a "room of a thousand moons" a blackened ceiling ponders a complex nighttime universe of celestial spheres, and the floor responds to the light cast with a series of circular wool rugs. In between, cotton-upholstered walls with neat rows of French nails hold together an eclectic period mix of furnishings and round lamps. Design: Carlos Aparicio and Jacqueline Coumans, courtesy of American Hospital of Paris French Designer Showhouse; Photo: Phillip H. Ennis

Bedroom
details

Futons from Japan, fluffy down-filled duvets from Scandinavia, and gauzy netting that was once necessary protection against mosquitoes in the tropics are some of the international stuff eclectic dreams are made of. Whether a rustic hideaway or a voluptuous boudoir, an expression of rugged individualism or an enchanted children's room, the eclectic sleep space thrives on unexpected variations on night tables and storage solutions and lots of souvenirs of personal history.

Bali Hai

A Balinese bed conjures up an instant aura of tropical romance around which the entire decor of the bedroom may be focused. Filmy veiling wrapped about almost any canopy bed, colorful batik fabrics fashioned into a bedspread, and several plump pillows do the trick.

The Missing Link

Textiles can be mixed with extreme abandon these days as long as something in their colors and textures weaves a certain relationship among them. Here, the trellis pattern—sometimes brash, sometimes subtle—links all fabrics and the rug.

Out of Africa

Alluringly creative signature touches can be achieved through groupings of ethnic jewelry, woven folk art, and handcarved travel knickknacks. They add not just color and pattern to a bedroom but delve into the texture of a sophisticated international sensibility.

Love of Nature

In lieu of the standard night table, a weathered tree trunk next to the bed infuses the room with a personal, eclectic, outdoorsy feeling, especially interesting when contrasted by a modern lamp.

Personal Statements

The creative process atop and above a simple dressing table can give a bedroom individual expression. Note how by hanging one mirror on ribbons the eye is carried to the quite dissimilar second mirror and the charmingly stacked family photographs and personal effects. **Design: Mark Hampton; Photo: Stan Rumbough**

Material World

Raw elements often supply quiet strength and textural contrast. Here a thoroughly novel side table of alternating bricks and flagstone underlines the rich variety of natural and manmade materials incorporated in the bedroom's careful design.

Picture Puzzle

Hanging assorted paintings for maximum impact requires certain cohesive elements. Thematic kinship—here, music—can be a unifying factor. Using similar frames can be another. Place paintings close together and square them off as if they were one large canvas. Place the center of the grouping at eye level.

Bandbox Perfect

Finishing touches are everything in this stylish night-and-day space. Note the meticulously draped and tailored daybed, subtly luxe fabrics, and dressmaker detailed pillows. Orderly rows of square French tacks create further refinement and interesting delineation of wall space.

Eastern Exposure

When East meets West in the eclectic bedroom, curtains matching bedcovers, which work so well in traditional bedrooms, give way to the serene simplicity of Asian reed window shades. These enhance the plain beauty of classic American country windows. Design: Barbara Colman; Photo: Peter Jaquith

Desk Set

See-through furnishings in natural and synthetic juxtapositions engender clever eclectic effects in limited spaces. A Lucite desk with a brown leather drawer fits the bill with such romantic accents as a crystal lamp, a bowl of roses, a cherished violin, and a handsome antique chair.

Directory of Designers, Manufacturers, and Photographers

*Designers and Manufacturers*s

Carlos Aparicio
30 East 67th Street
New York, NY 10021

Marcy Balk
44 West 76th Street #1
New York, NY 10023

Brian Murphy
BAM Design
147 Ω W. Channel Rd.
Santa Monica, CA 90404

David Barrett, FASID
131 East 71st Street
New York, NY 10021

Ben Baxt
Baxt Associates
20 Vesey Street Suite 900
New York, NY 10007

Thomas Beeton
723 Ω North Al Cienega
Los Angeles, CA 90069

Roberto Bergero
4 Rue St. Gilles
75004 Paris, France

Lise Davis Design at James Billings
Antiques and Interiors
34 Charles Street
Boston, MA

Debra A. Blair
Blair Design Associates Inc.
315 West 78th St.
New York, NY 10024

Thomas Britt
136 East 57th Street
New York, NY 10022

Cameron Cameron & Taylor Design
Associates
204 Columbia Heights
Brooklyn, NY 11201

Cynthia Clark Interiors
P.O. Box 714
North Hampton, NH 03862

Barbara Colman
Covington/ Colman
14 Imperial Place
Providence, RI 02903

Denis Colomb Interior Designer
1501 Third Avenue
New York, NY 10028

Jacqueline Coumans
21 East 92nd Street
New York, NY 10028

Robert Couturier
138 West 25th Street
New York, NY 10001

Carlos Alberto Cruz
Santiago, Chile

Martine Murat
Carocim Tile, U.S.A.
2008 Sepulveda Blvd.
Los Angeles, CA

Cullman & Kravis, Inc.
Interior Decoration for Collectors of Fine
Art and Antiques
790 Madison Avenue
New York, NY 10021

Billy Cunningham
140 Seventh Avenue Apt 4C
New York, NY 10011

Gerard Dalmon
Neotu Gallery
409 West 44th Street
New York, NY 10036

Jamie Drake
Drake Design Associates
140 East 56th Street
New York, NY 10022

Loren Dunlap, Artist
PO Box 332
Sagaponack, NY 11962

Tony Duquette,Designer
1354 Dawnbridge Drive
Beverly Hills, CA 90210

Beverly Ellsley
175 Post Road, West
Westport, CT 06880

Jeremy Railfon
Entertainment Design Corp.
1344 Fourth Street
Santa Monica, CA 90401

Susan Federman Interior Design
250 Laurel Street
Suite 301
San Francisco, CA 94118

Richard Fitzgerald & Company, Inc.
576 Boylston St.
Boston, MA

Rena Fortagang
27 Forest Avenue
Locust Valley, NY 11560

Ellen Genauer & Lenore Gold
515 E 72nd Street
New York, NY 10021

Jacques Grange
118, rue Faubourg Saint HonrE
75008 Paris, France

Haman & Yaw Architects
210 S. Galena, Suite 24
Aspen, CO 81811

Eddie E. Harris
Harris-Sanders Interior Design
2401 San Felipe
Houston, TX 77019

Kathy Irwin
1192 Park Avenue
New York, NY 10128

Jeanne- Aelia Desparmet - Hart
JADH Interior Design
19 Roosevelt Avenue
Larchmond, NY 10538

Jake Victor & Jennifer Ellenberg
Jake Victor Associates
34 West Ninth Street
New York, NY 10011

Annie Kelly
2074 Watsonia Terrace
Los Angeles, CA 90068

Sandra Killough
115 East 90th Street
New York, NY 10128

Kitchens Bedrooms Bathrooms Magazine
Equitable House
Lyon Road
Harrow HA12EW
United Kingdom

Diane Knight Interiors
111 Birch Rd.
Locust Valley, NY 11560

Ellen Lemer Korny
10490 Charing Cross Road
Los Angeles, CA 90024

Laurence Kriegel
710 Broadway
New York, NY 10003

Ann Lenox
Partners in Design
86 Walnut Street
Newton Centre, MA 02159

Martin Kuckly
Kuckly Associates, Inc.
509 East 74th Street
New York, NY 10021

Lalique North America, Inc
41 Madison Avenue
New York, NY 10010

Dominique Lange/Lisa Wassong
Decorative Painters
294 Rocktown - Lambertville Rd.
Lambertville, New Jersey 08530-3303
   with
Hut-Sach Studio
Architects
55 Crosby Street
New York, NY 10012

Larry Laslo
127 East 64th Street
New York, NY 10021

Michael Davies and Andrew Logan
Logan Davies
The Glass House
Melior Place
London SE13QP
England

Veronique Loubet
140 Campbell Street
Boston, MA 02119

Made Wijaya Design
c/o Michael White
341 Dahah Road
Singapore

Robert Madey Architecture
1175 Montauk Highway
West Islip, New York 11795

Roger Prigent
Malmaison Antiques
253 E. 74th Street
New York, NY 10021

Dave Marlow
Building 421 AABC
Aspen, CO 81611

Manuel Mestre Architect
Reforma 2009
Mexico D.F. 11000

Niu Miyasato
130 West 79th Street
New York, NY 10024

Juan Pablo Molyneux
J. P. Molyneux Studio Ltd.
29 East 69th Street
New York, NY 10021

Miss Brett Nestler
350 E. 79th Street
New York, NY 10021

Timothy J. Oldfield, Architect
207 Sandy Pond Rd.
Lincoln, MA 01773

Polly Osborne
Osborne Erickson Architects
1833 Stanford St.
Santa Monica, CA 90404

Josef Pricci Interiors
737 Park Avenue
New York, NY 10021

Charles Riley Designer
45 Fifth Avenue
New York, NY 10003

John Copeland
Robinson Gardens
1008 Elder Drive
Bel Air, CA 90210

Ann Fox
Room Service
4354 Lovers Lane
Dallas, TX 75225

Marilyn H. Rose Interiors
4 Birch Hill Rd.
Locust Valley, NY 11560

Leopoldo Rosati Interior Architecture
& Design
300 East 40th Street, Suite 10-S
New York, NY 10016

John F. Saladino
Saladino Group, Inc.
200 Lexington Avenue Suite 1600
New York, NY 10016

Odile de Schietere
Odile de S.
European Interior Design
979 Third Avenue, Suite 1640
New York, NY 10022

David Scott
151 East 80th Street #5c
New York, NY 10021

Teri Seidman Interiors
150East 61st Street
New York, NY 10021

Raphael Serrano
1551 Meridich Avenue
Miami, Fl

Tim Street-Porter
2074 Watsonia Terrace
Hollywood, CA 90068

Larry Total Design
2912 Colorado Avenue #201
Santa Monica, CA 90404

Adrienne Vittadini
575 Seventh Avenue
New York, NY 10018

Aman waha Indonesia
Aman Design Department
Hong Kong Headquarters

Marshall Watson Interiors, Ltd.
105 West 72nd Street 9B
New York, NY 10023

Waterworks
29 park Avenue
Danbury, CT 06810

John Widdicomb company
601 Fifth Street NW
Grand Rapids, MI 49504-5197

Hutton Wilkinson
1910 Outpost Drive
Los Angeles, CA 90068

Mark Wilkinson
Mark Wilkinson Furniture Limited
Overton House, High Street
Bromhanu, Chippenham
Wilshire, UK SN152HA

Eleanor Windman
200 East 57th Street Apt. 4F
New York, NY 10022

Virginia Witbeck
P.O. Box 962
Bridgehampton, NY 11932